初中英语戏剧读本

Sai Weng and His Horse
塞翁失马

James Bean & Gillian Flaherty

上海教育出版社
SHANGHAI EDUCATIONAL PUBLISHING HOUSE

Summary
故事概要

Sai Weng and his son kept horses near the country's border. One day, a horse went missing. They could not find her. They saw tracks leading to the border, where it was too dangerous to go. Sai Weng accepted that the horse was lost. Neighbours came to say how sorry they were about this. But Sai Weng told them that bad luck can sometimes change to good luck.

Months later, the horse returned, bringing with her another horse. The neighbours came to see the horse, telling Sai Weng how lucky he was. But Sai Weng said good luck sometimes changes to bad.

One day Sai Weng's son fell off the new horse. He broke his leg and could not walk. He said his life was ruined. The neighbours came to say how sorry they were. But Sai Weng said the accident might not be so bad — bad luck sometimes changes to good.

War broke out. A soldier arrived. All the young men in the country had to join the army. Sai Weng's son could not go, because he could not walk.

Many young men died in the war, but Sai Weng's son was safe. Sai Weng told him that bad luck sometimes changes to good luck, and good luck sometimes changes to bad.

Characters
主要角色

Sai Weng

Sai Weng's Son

Li, Sai Weng's servant

Soldier

Neighbours

Act 1

Narrator:
This is the story of Sai Weng, a wise, old man. He and his son lived out on the plain, near the country's border. They kept horses and rode them every day. They took good care of their horses.

Sai Weng's Son:
Good morning, Father.

Sai Weng:
Good morning, my son. Have you fed the horses?

Sai Weng's Son:
Yes, Father. I've given them hay and now they are in the fields.

Sai Weng:
You are a great help to me, Son. Oh, here comes our servant, Li.

Li enters quickly. He looks worried.

Li:

Good morning, Master. Come quickly! One of your finest horses has gone missing!

Sai Weng:

Gone missing? Which horse?

Li:

The one with the white star on her forehead.

Sai Weng's Son:

Oh, no! That's Starlight! She's my favourite horse. We must find her.

Sai Weng:

Yes, we must. Let's go and look straight away.

Narrator:

Sai Weng and his son and his servant started to search for the missing horse. They rode around the countryside for hours and hours. But they could not find her anywhere. Then Sai Weng's son saw some horse tracks on the ground. The tracks led towards the border.

Sai Weng's Son:

Father, we must follow these tracks to find Starlight!

Sai Weng:

No, my son. We can't do that. The tracks lead towards the border. It's too dangerous to go there. We'll never see Starlight again.

Narrator:

The news of this misfortune soon travelled everywhere. Many friends and neighbours came to visit Sai Weng.

Neighbour 1:

Sai Weng, I'm so sorry to hear about your bad luck.

Neighbour 2:

Yes, what a disaster for you!

Sai Weng:

Thank you, friends, for your concern. But I'm not too worried.

Neighbour 3:

What on earth do you mean? You've lost a valuable horse!

Neighbour 4:

Don't you think that's bad luck?

Sai Weng:

Calm down, my friends. Don't be so upset. It may not be so bad. Remember, bad luck can change to good luck!

Act 2

Narrator:

Two months passed. They kept searching but there was no sign of the missing horse. Sai Weng's son was very sad.

Sai Weng's Son:

I miss Starlight very much. She was a beautiful horse.

Sai Weng:
Oh, Son, it's sad, but you must accept that the horse has gone. You must not think about it all the time. Let's get back to work. We have to make a living.

Sai Weng's Son:
I'll get back to work, but I'll never stop looking for Starlight.

Narrator:

Then, one day Sai Weng's son saw something in the distance. It was a horse coming across the plain.

Sai Weng's Son:

Oh, Father, Father, look! It's Starlight. She's coming back.

Sai Weng:

Look more closely, Son. That's not one horse — there are two horses!

Sai Weng's Son:

You're right! Look! Starlight has a friend. It's a fine big horse.

The two horses enter.

Sai Weng:

They must have come back across the border. They have travelled a long way. Quick, Li! Get them some water and hay.

Li:

Yes, Master. I'll go right away. Oh, what a happy day!

The servant fetches water and hay for the horses.

Narrator:

The news of this great fortune travelled fast. Friends and neighbours came to visit. They wanted to see the fine new horse.

The neighbours enter and they all crowd around the horses, admiring them.

Neighbour 1:

Sai Weng, your fortune has changed. You have gained a fine big horse!

Neighbour 2:

You're a lucky man, Sai Weng. First you lost one horse, but then you got two horses back!

Neighbour 3:

And the new horse is magnificent!

Sai Weng's Son:

I'm so happy that Starlight is back. And we are so lucky to have this new horse too. Let's call him Lucky!

Neighbour 4:

That's the perfect name.

Neighbour 1:

Lucky horse! Lucky Sai Weng!

Sai Weng:

Why are you all so certain that this horse is lucky? He might bring us bad luck. Remember, good luck can sometimes change to bad luck.

Act 3

Narrator:

Sai Weng's son was so happy with his fine new horse. He took good care of Lucky and he rode him all the time.

Sai Weng's son enters, riding the new horse.

Sai Weng's Son:

Look at me! I'm riding on a fine horse.

Li:

Yes, you look dashing on that horse.

Sai Weng's Son:

Look out, Li! Here I come! Ha, ha!

Li:

Be careful, Master. Don't go too fast.

Narrator:

The young man galloped around carelessly. When Li told him to be careful, he didn't listen.

Sai Weng's Son:

I'm brave and fearless, not careful! Come on, Lucky! Let's go!

Sai Weng's son falls off the horse. He immediately cries out in pain as he has hurt his leg.

Li:

Oh, no! He's fallen off!

Li runs to Sai Weng's son, looking very worried.

Master, are you alright?

Sai Weng's Son:

Aaahhh! My leg!

Li:

Don't move. I'll get your father.

Li runs off, looking worried.

Sai Weng's Son:

Oh, my leg is so painful. What if it's broken?

Sai Weng and Li enter in a hurry.

Sai Weng:

My son, what have you done?

Sai Weng's Son:

I fell from Lucky and now I think my leg is broken.

Sai Weng:

Let me see.

Sai Weng looks carefully at his son's injured leg.

Sai Weng:

Yes, it looks bad. Help me, Li. We must take him back to the house.

Sai Weng's Son:

Father, I'm sorry. I was foolish. I rode too fast.

Sai Weng:

Don't worry about that now, Son. We must look after your leg right away.

Li helps Sai Weng carry his son off.

Narrator:

The young man's leg was broken and he could not walk. Sai Weng's friends and neighbours heard about this and came to visit.

Neighbour 1:

Sai Weng, I'm sorry to hear your terrible news.

Neighbour 2:

They say your son will never walk again. More bad luck!

Sai Weng's Son:

I have been foolish. My life is ruined.

Sai Weng:

Never talk like that again, Son. You're lucky to be alive.

Neighbour 3:

But he'll never walk again! What a disaster!

Neighbour 4:

Now he can't help you with all the work.

Sai Weng:

Thank you, friends, for your concern. But why are you all so worried? This accident might bring us good luck in the future. Remember, bad luck can sometimes change to good luck.

Act 4

Narrator:

A year went by, and the country was at war. One day a soldier arrived.

A soldier knocks on the door.

Soldier:

Open up!

Li:

What's the matter?

Soldier:

I'm from the army. Don't you know we're at war? I'm looking for young men to join up. We need more soldiers. I hope there are some strong young men here.

Li:

Wait a moment, please. I'll go and get the master, Sai Weng.

Li exits. The soldier looks around at the house and yard while he waits.

Sai Weng enters.

Sai Weng:

How can I help you, Sir?

Soldier:

I'm looking for young men to join the army. Do you have any strong young men here?

Sai Weng:

No, sir. I cannot help you. There's no one like that here.

Soldier:

Don't you have a son? All the young men in the country must join the army. We're at war!

Sai Weng:

I do, but —

Soldier:

Bring him here at once!

Sai Weng:

But he can't walk. He broke his leg.

Soldier:

Broke his leg? Show me! Where is he?

Sai Weng:

You'd better follow me. He's in the garden.

They walk to the garden where Sai Weng's son is sitting.

Sai Weng:
This is my son.

Soldier:
Stand up, young man! You're going to be a soldier.

Sai Weng's Son:
I don't understand. What do you mean?

Soldier:
Don't you know we're at war?
Our country needs you.
Come with me!

Sai Weng's Son:
Sorry, Sir. I can't go.
I can't even stand up.

Sai Weng:
You see, he fell from a horse and broke his leg. Although he wants to be a soldier, he cannot be one.

Soldier:
Well then, he's no good to me. Good day!

The soldier exits angrily.

Narrator:

The war went on for several years and many soldiers died. Many families lost their sons.

Sai Weng:

You are alive, my son, when many of our young men are dead. You thought your life was ruined, but in fact it was saved. We have had good luck and bad luck. But nothing was as it seemed. You see, bad luck can sometimes change to good luck, and good luck can sometimes change to bad luck. What will the future bring? Who knows?

The End

Retell the story
复述故事

Act 1
- one horse missing
- horse tracks on the ground
- bad luck can change to good luck

Act 2
- get back to work
- come back
- two horses
- good luck can change to bad luck

Act 3
- ride the new horse all the time
- fall off the horse
- break his leg
- bad luck can change to good luck

Act 4
- at war
- look for young men to join up
- cannot walk
- What will the future bring? Who knows?

Think and answer
问题与思考

1. Why didn't Sai Weng go to look for Starlight at first?
2. How did Sai Weng feel when he got Starlight back again?
3. Was Sai Weng's son lucky or not? Why?
4. What do you think of Sai Weng?

词汇与表达

单词

accept	v. 接受	gain	v. 获得
admire	v. 赞赏	gallop	v. 飞驰
border	n. 边；边界	immediately	adv. 立即；马上
companion	n. 同伴	injure	v. 伤害；使受伤
concern	n. 关心	misfortune	n. 不幸的事
crowd	v. 挤满；聚集	magnificent	adj. 壮丽的；伟大的
certain	adj. 确定的；肯定的	plain	n. 平原；广阔的区域
disaster	n. 灾难	ruin	v. 破坏；毁灭
dashing	adj. 自信的；潇洒的	several	adj. 几个的；数个的
forehead	n. 额；前额	track	n. 痕迹；踪迹
follow	v. 跟随；跟着	upset	adj. 心烦的；混乱的
fetch	v. 取来；接来	valuable	adj. 贵重的；宝贵的
fearless	adj. 无畏的；勇敢的	yard	n. 院子

短语

all the time	总是	hear about	听说
at war	在战争中	in the distance	远处
break out	爆发	join the army	参军；入伍
bring sb. sth.	把某物带给某人	keep doing	持续做
cry out	呼喊；尖叫	make a living	维持生活
carry off	抬走	no sign of	没有……的迹象
fall off	摔下	straight away	立刻
get back to	回到……		

第一幕：

旁白：这是关于塞翁的故事。他是一位有智慧的老人。他和他的儿子住在边境附近的平原上。他们每天在那里养马、骑马，悉心照料着他们的马。

塞翁之子：父亲，早上好。

塞翁：早上好啊，我的儿子。你喂过马了吗？

塞翁之子：是的，父亲。我已经喂过草料，他们现在已经在牧场了。

塞翁：你真是我的好帮手啊，儿子。哦，我们的家仆老李来了。

老李迅速上场。他看上去忧心忡忡。

老李：老爷，早上好。快来！您最好的马中有一匹不见了！

塞翁：不见了？哪匹马？

老李：额头上有白色星星斑纹的那匹。

塞翁之子：哦不！是星光！她是我最喜欢的马。我们必须把她找回来。

塞翁：是的，必须找回来。我们马上就去。

旁白：塞翁、他的儿子和家仆开始寻找走丢的马。他们在村野里寻找了好久，但是哪儿也找不到星光。这时，塞翁的儿子看见地上有一些马蹄的印迹。这些印迹朝着边境外去了。

塞翁之子：父亲，我们必须循着这些印迹找到星光。

塞翁：不，我的儿子。我们不能那么做。这些印迹朝着边境外去了。去那儿太危险了。恐怕我们再也见不到星光了。

旁白：这个不幸的消息很快就传遍了。许多朋友和邻居都来安慰塞翁。

邻居1：塞翁，听到这个坏消息真是太遗憾了。

邻居2：是啊，对你来说真是一场灾难啊！

塞翁：朋友们，感谢你们的关心。但我不是非常担心。

邻居3：你的意思是？你可是丢了一匹良驹啊！

邻居4：你不觉得这是噩运吗？

塞翁：冷静点，我的朋友们。不用那么难过。也许没有那么糟。记住，噩运可能会变成好运！

第二幕

旁白：两个月过去了。他们仍然在寻找，却没有那匹丢失的马的任何踪影。塞翁的儿子非常伤心。

塞翁之子：我非常想念星光。她是一匹非常漂亮的马。

塞翁：哦，儿子啊，这是件伤心事，但是你必须接受马已经丢了的事实。你不能总是想着这件事情。我们得回到工作中去。我们还要生活的。

塞翁之子：我会回去工作的，但我不会停止寻找星光。

旁白：后来，有一天，塞翁的儿子看到远处有什么东西。是一匹马正在穿越平原。

塞翁之子：哦，父亲，父亲，快看！是星光。她回来了。

塞翁：再仔细看看，儿子。不只一匹马，是两匹！

塞翁之子：您说得对！看！星光带了一个朋友。一匹高大的骏马。

两匹马出场。

塞翁：他们一定是穿越边境回来的。他们经历了漫长的旅途。快点，老李！拿些

　　　　水和干草来。
　　老李：好的，老爷。我马上就去。哦，真是开心的一天！
家仆取来了水和干草喂两匹马。
　　旁白：这个好消息很快传开了。朋友和邻居们都来拜访。他们想看看那匹新来的骏马。
邻居们出场，他们围在马儿边上，赞赏他们。
　　邻居1：塞翁啊，你转运了。你多得了一匹良驹啊！
　　邻居2：你真是幸运啊，塞翁。你先是丢了一匹马，但是现在你得回了两匹！
　　邻居3：这匹新来的马真棒！
　　塞翁之子：星光回来，我太高兴了。能得到这匹新的马，我们也是很幸运。就叫他幸运吧！
　　邻居4：真是个好名字。
　　邻居1：好运之马！好运塞翁！
　　塞翁：为什么你们那么确定这匹马是幸运的？也许他会给我们带来噩运。记住，好运有时候也会变成噩运。

第三幕

　　旁白：塞翁的儿子因为得到了新的良驹而高兴不已。他悉心照顾幸运，总是骑他外出。
塞翁之子出场，骑着那匹新马。
　　塞翁之子：看我！我正骑着一匹骏马呢。
　　老李：是啊，您骑这马看上去威风凛凛啊。
　　塞翁之子：快看，老李！我来啦！哈哈！
　　老李：小心点，少爷。别骑太快。
　　旁白：年轻人毫不在意地一路疾驰。老李提醒他要小心，他根本听不进去。
　　塞翁之子：我可是非常勇敢，无所畏惧的，别担心！幸运，加油！快跑！
塞翁之子从马上摔了下来。他立刻因为剧痛大叫起来，他摔伤了腿。
　　老李：哦，不！少爷摔下来了！
老李满脸焦急地朝塞翁的儿子跑去。
　　　　少爷，您没事吧？
　　塞翁之子：啊！我的腿！
　　老李：别动。我去叫老爷。
老李心急火燎地跑回家去。
　　塞翁之子：哦，我的腿好痛。是不是断了？
塞翁和老李急急忙忙地出场。
　　塞翁：我的儿子，你怎么样了？
　　塞翁之子：我从幸运上摔了下来，我觉得我的腿摔断了。
　　塞翁：让我看看。
塞翁仔细查看了他儿子受伤的腿。
　　塞翁：哎，看上去很糟。帮我一下，老李。我们必须把他背回家里去。
　　塞翁之子：对不起，父亲。我太蠢了。我骑得太快了。
　　塞翁：别担心了，儿子。我们必须立刻治疗你的腿。
老李帮着塞翁背走了他的儿子。
　　旁白：年轻人的腿摔断了，他不能走路了。塞翁的朋友和邻居们听说了这个消

息，都来慰问。
邻居1：塞翁，很抱歉听到这个噩耗。
邻居2：听说你儿子再也不能走路了。真是太不幸了！
塞翁之子：我真是傻。我的生活被毁了。
塞翁：儿子，别再这样说。能活着就是幸运的。
邻居3：但他再也不能走路了！真是大难啊！
邻居4：现在他也不能帮我们干活了。

P21 塞翁：谢谢你们的关心，朋友们。但是你们为什么都如此担忧？也许这个意外在将来会给我们带来好运。记住，噩运有时候也会变成好运。

P22 **第四幕**

旁白：一年后，战争爆发。一天，来了一个士兵。
士兵敲门。
士兵：开门！
老李：有什么事？
士兵：我从部队来。你知道我们都在打仗吗？我在寻找年轻人参军。我们需要更多的士兵。希望这里有强壮的年轻人。
老李：请稍等。我去叫我家老爷，塞翁。
老李退场。士兵一边等待，一边环视房子和院子。

P23 *塞翁出场。*
塞翁：军爷，有什么需要我们帮忙的吗？
士兵：我在寻找年轻男子参军。你家有强壮的年轻男子吗？
塞翁：没有，军爷。我帮不上忙了。我们这里没有这样的人。

P24 士兵：你不是有个儿子吗？全国所有的年轻男子都要参军。我们正在打仗！
塞翁：我是有一个儿子，但是——
士兵：立刻把他带过来！
塞翁：但是他不能走路。他摔断了腿。
士兵：摔断了腿？让我看看！他在哪里？
塞翁：请随我来。他在园子里。

P25 *他们走进园子，塞翁的儿子正坐在那里。*
塞翁：这就是我的儿子。
士兵：年轻人，站起来！你就要成为一名士兵了。
塞翁之子：我不明白。你什么意思？
士兵：你不知道我们正在打仗吗？国家需要你。跟我走吧！
塞翁之子：对不起，军爷。我走不了。我甚至都站不起来。

P26 塞翁：您看，他从马上摔下来，摔断了腿。虽然他也想当一名士兵，但是他不能。
士兵：好吧，他没什么用了。再见！
士兵怒气冲冲地离开。

P27 旁白：战争持续了多年，许多士兵都牺牲了。许多家庭失去了他们的孩子。
塞翁：好多年轻人都死了，而你还活着，我的儿子。你曾经觉得你的生活被毁了，但事实上却是得救了。我们时而有好运，时而有噩运。但事情不是都如表面所见。你看，噩运有时会变成好运，而好运有时也会变成噩运。未来会怎样？又有谁会知道？

剧终